# SECONDARY SCHOOL
## AND
## HOW TO SURVIVE IT

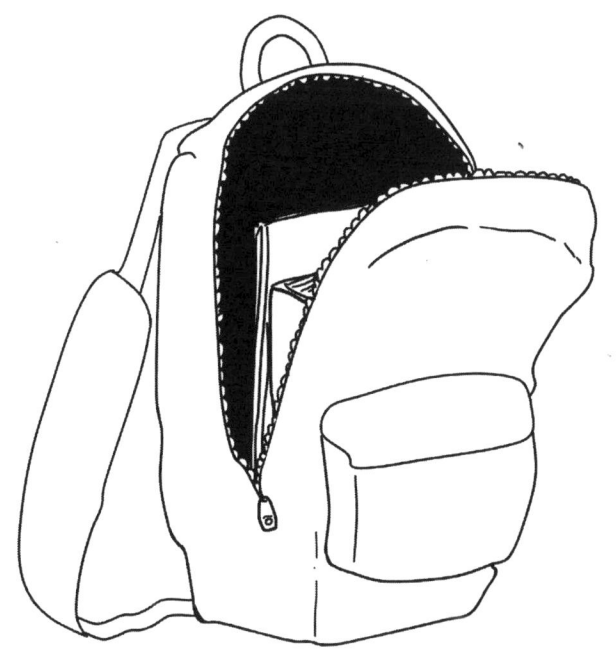

*Written and illustrated by*
# INDIGO HAYNES

Copyright @ Indigo Haynes 2019, 2020

All rights reserved.
Published by Thimblerig Books

**A NEW REVISED EDITION 2020**

The moral right of the author has been asserted.
No part of this book can be reproduced or transferred by any means without the express written permission of the author.

ISBN: 9781983060823

# TEXT & ILLUSTRATIONS

## Indigo Haynes

Indigo Haynes is a British teen writer and artist with a special interest in manga and anime. She's a writer-illustrator-animator, with a YouTube animation channel and work featured in anime zines. As well as art, Indigo is also passionate about politics, and campaigns for action against climate change.

# EDITING & FORMATTING

## Dylan Haynes and Jane Holland

# Contents

INTRODUCTION
TO BEDHAIR OR NOT BEDHAIR
FRIENDS 'N' FIENDS
YOUR TYPICAL SCHOOLFRIEND TYPES
SCHOOLWORK: THE STUDY BUDDY MOMENT
MY TOP GUIDE FOR WRIGGLING OUT OF TROUBLE
HAIRY STYLES
TO SPORT OR NOT TO SPORT – SORRY, NO CHOICE
BULLYING
INDIGO'S GUIDE TO TEACHERS: ABSOLUTE EDUCATORS
FRIENDSHIP GROUPS
THE INCREDIBLE JOURNEY
KEEPING UP WITH THE –ISMS
AFTERWORD– A FEW LAST TIPS

# What's this book about?

**The teenage years:** a mish-mash of hormones, frustration, and just trying to make it to the end of the school year. Each day a sickening drudge on to the next twenty-four hour cycle while the eternal question lingers in your weary brain: 'Is school food really the remains of aliens who run the school instead of teachers?'

Sound familiar?

This handbook is a guide to life at school written entirely by me, Indigo, a Year 9 prisoner, oops, I mean, student at secondary school. My guide is crammed full of wacky, funny, and yet totally realistic clues on how to survive up to seven long years at secondary school too. You may even enjoy school by the end of it...

*Indigo Haynes*

# WARNING!

Everything in this book is based on my experience, and if you find yourself in a situation which I haven't encountered, I'm not sure how much I can help… but I'm sure that *something* in this book will help you!

You'll have ups and downs, and you will have to endure them all. But you won't get anything if you don't work for it! You can have as many friends as you want who will support you if you can really open up to people, and you'll have great grades too if you study hard.

If you are naturally shy, then get out there! Venture out of your comfort zone, because the only things you'll truly regret when you're older will be the things you were too scared to do when you were younger.

Are you prepared for the challenge? Are you prepared to achieve your dreams, and get through secondary school intact?

If so, then dive right in … !!!

# STAY SAFE

If you're reading this in the dreaded Age of Coronavirus, please stay safe!

Follow your school's protocol for social distancing, keep within your class or peer group 'bubble', wash your hands with soap and water for at least 30 seconds – no skimping! – and try to use hand gel or sanitizer – who knew that was a serious thing before 2020? – with at least 60% alcohol to kill germs, if you can't get to a sink or soap and water. Avoid touching anything you don't have to, especially on the bus. Avoid touching your face too.

So, that's …

WEAR A MASK

DON'T STAND TOO CLOSE TO OTHER PEOPLE

WASH HANDS WITH SOAP FOR 30 SECONDS

USE HAND SANITISER

STAY IN YOUR CLASS 'BUBBLE' IF DIRECTED

AVOID TOUCHING YOUR FACE

# WASH YOUR HANDS

# TO BEDHAIR OR NOT TO BEDHAIR

## HOW TO DRAG YOURSELF TO SCHOOL IN THE MORNINGS

Not a morning person? Don't worry, you won't become one until you're at least forty! When I wake up in the morning, don't know about you, but I'm always groggy and tired. I just want to stay in bed for as long as possible.

My hair looks like a cross between Medusa and the gooey stuff that clogs up bathroom plugholes, my alarm is blaring, and often just getting up to turn it off involves tripping over onto my face because of the insane maze of mess on my floor.

But the first step toward conquering secondary school is waking up early, because it gives you time to make it look like you care. Trust me on this. Looking like you care impresses teachers and makes them think of you as an exemplary student.

# ROCK YOUR UNIFORM ...

Anyone would prefer wearing their own clothes to the grim outfits schoolchildren are forced into for our teachers' amusement. Teachers like to see us not only wearing the correct uniform, but it needs to be CLEAN too.

Sadly, sticking to the rules of your uniform code is very important if you want to survive secondary school. Why? Because teachers like to see the uniform code working.

And if your teachers don't like you, because you don't look the same as everyone else, they will make your life very unpleasant and you won't have their support.

You can't survive secondary school without the support of at least one teacher. It's the hard truth.

# NO RUSSIAN!

Finally, don't rush – it makes you look disorganised and people are less likely to respect you. Respect is the end goal, so messing it up at the very beginning isn't exactly ideal.

Waking up early gives you enough time to make sure you have everything you need, and you can organise your outfit.

An even better way to do it is to organise your clothes the night before, so you don't make choices while you're tired in the morning.

Your bag is also important.

You will have a lot more things to bring to school with you than usually if you're really serious about ruling the school, so I recommend a large bag to fit everything in.

# WHAT'S YOUR BAG?

The style of bag is important and getting it wrong can be very embarrassing. Avoid cartoon character school bags, they look a bit too 'primary school' but equally say no to a business-like, leather briefcase if you can.

You're not a city exec, and besides, you need a side pocket for your water bottle, and sturdy straps, and it ought to be at least vaguely waterproof for all those times you get stuck waiting in the rain when your parents don't turn up or the bus is late …

When in doubt, a comfortable rucksack is the way to go. So, if you're ready, let's start with the obvious, number one ingredient for your new school bag … No, not a choc bar or bag of crisps.. I meant, sadly, your pencil case.

# PENCIL CASE S-ENSHELLS
*(Sorry ...)*

You don't want to be that one doofus who's always asking for a pencil in class – it'll eventually make you unpopular, especially with your teachers. So if you can afford it, try to make sure you have anything in that pencil case you could ever want, pens, pencils, rubbers, rulers ...

Highlighters and sharpeners are important, too. You might want a mini-calculator and some dinky little toys to fiddle with while that annoying new supply teacher is droning on and on ... Oops, I mean, teaching.

And your phone. If you've got one. But keep it on silent. Unless you want it confiscated. You'll soon learn which teachers will snatch it from your sweaty paws as soon as you so much as glance at Snapchat, and which teachers won't even notice you having an in-depth convo with your mate in Double Science.

# ERM… WHICH BOOK AGAIN?

Check your schedule the night before and organise all the books you have to bring to your classes. These will likely be the heaviest things in your bag, so don't carry any you don't need. Not unless you're part-camel, that is.

But in the same way never leave a book behind simply because you can't be bothered to hunt for it under your bed, or it's too heavy. Forgetfulness is something your teachers will not appreciate. Their bad, of course. But we have to play the game.

# FUD TIME

Unless your food serves the best grub in the universe, I'm willing to bet it's more unhealthy than healthy. Chips, sausage rolls, more chips …

Just getting through the school day is tiring, and even if you grab a tasty hot meal in the middle of the day, you'll need a snack or two to help you through break times and other 'OMG, I'm exhausted' moments. Don't rely on choccies and crisps to keep you going though. These may be yummy, but they'll probably end up giving you a sugar rush.

So it's a great idea to take your own healthy pick-me-up food to school if possible, especially an apple or banana, or a few, non-sugary cereal snack bars, for those moments when your energy is flagging and you've got double PE next!

# FRIENDS AND FIENDS

# OR, WHO YOU'LL MEET AT THE SCHOOL FACE

## FIRST, MAKE A PIE CHART

Most people in schools can be put into categories. Yes, really. You can make a graph with these people.

Or even a pie chart. Just don't try to eat one. Trust me on this. Pupil pie charts can be pretty indigestible.

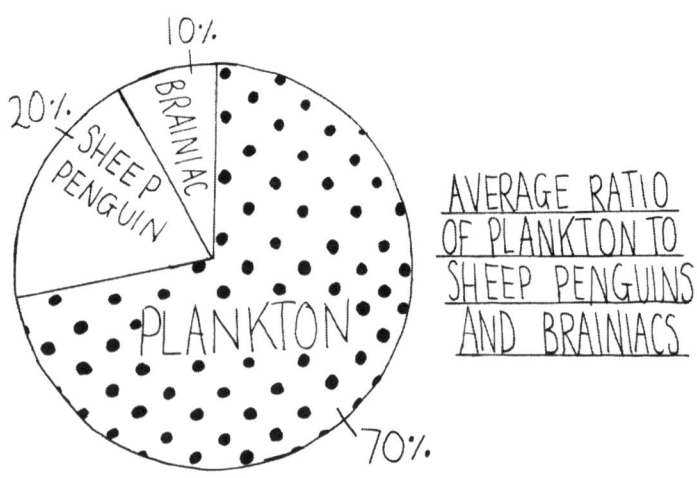

# SHEEP PENGUINS

A 'sheep penguin' is simply a very popular person who does exactly what everyone else is doing (like a sheep) and walks around with a giant group of friends, huddled together (like penguins).

Sheep penguins can be girls or boys, and they usually have styled hair, don't abide by the rules of the school uniform, and have a smug or laid-back attitude.

They are in the middle of every crazy dating drama and they are usually the most sought-after people in the school.

# SHEEP PENGUINS

No, a 'sheep penguin' is not a bizarre cross between a sheep and a penguin. Sorry!

A sheep penguin is a deeply popular person who does exactly what everyone else is doing (like a sheep) and who never goes anywhere without a giant group of friends, huddled together (like penguins on an ice floe).

Sheep penguins can be girls or boys, and they usually have styled hair, don't abide by the rules of the school uniform, and have a smug or laid-back attitude. They're in the middle of every crazy dating drama, and are usually the most sought-after people in the school.

So how do you stand out against the rest of the people wanting to be their friends – and why should you want to in the first place? Sheep penguins are at the top of the pyramid, and they know everything about everyone. With them as your friends, you can survive school, truly.

Usually sheep penguins are only friends with other sheep penguins, so the only way to be friends with them without being a sheep penguin is to get on their radar. To do this you'll need the help of the next group of kids.

# BRAINIAC

A 'Brainiac' can usually be defined as someone in the top class, someone really clever. Brainiacs can be anything from as shy as a mouse to even being a popular sheep penguin.

Usually, it's easy to tell a Brainiac apart from other kids, but there are people who try to hide how clever they are so they can be popular, which makes it trickier.

Since Brainiacs are so clever, teachers don't tell them off as much. A Brainiac might wear their uniform wrong with their shirt untucked or their tie crooked, but no teacher would notice or care!

Of course, this makes it hard to tell a Brainiac from a sheep penguin.

You will need at least one Brainiac's help to achieve your goal in school, whatever it may be. If you are a Brainiac yourself, this will not be a problem.

But anyone can become a Brainiac if they really put their mind to it. You just have to get in the mindset for learning. You can do it, if you study. I have more on studying later, if you want some tips to getting into a study group…

Sheep penguins mainly use their connections to ask Brainiacs for help, since sheep penguins spend so much time going to parties and gossiping, they don't have time to study.

If you can find a subject a sheep penguin is bad at, but you are good at, then you can offer to tutor them.

# PLANKTON

Plankton are everywhere. They are those people in school who keep their heads down and out of trouble because they don't want to get involved in any drama.

You probably won't notice plankton, unless you are one.

The main goal of plankton is to get through the school year without too much drama.

In other words, they behave well and wear their school uniform perfectly, to avoid being noticed by teachers.

## "Hello, I'm plankton too ..."

If you ask a plankton what they want to be when they're older, all you'll get is a glare – but honestly, who can blame them?

Sometimes I'm so tired, all I can only think about the next school day, let alone what I'll be doing in the next decade!

So get out there and talk to plankton (even if you're one yourself). Introduce yourself and start a conversation. Once they've shared their deepest, darkest secrets, you can really begin to understand them and enjoy having them as a friend.

Honest.

# YOUR TYPICAL SCHOOLFRIEND TYPES

## THE HYPNOTIST

Everyone has that one friend, that one charming friend who has everyone wrapped around their finger. They look so sad; nobody can ever refuse them if they ask for something.

They are masterfully skilled in manipulation and have the ability to make their eyes well up with tears at any opportunity. If a hypnotist really wants something, they will usually get it.

# "Look into my eyes ..."

Most times, you will end up giving the Hypnotist whatever they want, because of their puppy-dog eyes. Not good, especially if they turn out to be treacherous. These people can completely ruin your reputation if they turn on you later. So choose your friends carefully!

On the other hand, it could prove a large advantage to have a friend like that to call on. Under their influence, a strict teacher could become more lenient and you could get invited to sheep-penguin parties when otherwise you might've been left off the invitation list.

You'll undoubtedly feel the urge to protect them from any sheep penguins willing to use them for their popularity. Either way, friends should be cherished, not used!

# SIR/LADY TALKALOT

Sir/Lady Talk-a-lot will continuously chatter like a robot with no off switch. They will talk non-stop and if you dare to butt in, you'll get an indignant sniff, followed by a glare, before the person continues on with their unflagging speech. If what they're saying is interesting, you may find yourself invested in their story. But the majority of the time they only talk about themselves and their own problems.

Either that or you'll find yourself sitting there and feeling stupid and inadequate as they complain about the fact that they were only 1 mark off full score in the maths test, or the fact that they didn't get an A** on their essay, merely an A*.

Usually, they have no idea that they're making you feel bad. If they let you get a word in edgeways, maybe you could inform them of that… Good luck with that! They're great to hang out with if you're at a loose end, but sometimes there are times when you just want peace and quiet.

# THE NOM-NOM-NOM

You're in the cafeteria. The sound of other students chatting with their friends is overpowering. Just as you're digging into a delicious turkey sandwich, you look up to see two hungry eyes staring at you from the other side of the table.

This friend can eat anything and never turn into more of a stick figure. They just shrug off food like it's nothing. That of course means that they are never full. If you have so much as a crumb left on your plate, they will snatch it from you. The problems happen when it's more than just a crumb.

Soon, you'll have to bring extra food for your hungry friend. But that sets up for the dilemma of what to do when they're ill.

For the sake of not wasting food, you should hand out the snax to your other friends and let them share it between them – it can be a great opportunity to have a feast with your friends.

# LONGHAIRED MUSICIAN

This person isn't really a musician. They may not even have long hair. But that's what your friend wants to be. Though you can't blame them - this person loves music so much, it's only logical they'd want a career in it too. They live and breathe the latest tunes, their MP3 player is always playing and their eyes are always closed, inhaling the sweet, sweet music.

At least, except for the moments when they're trying to force their particular music tastes onto you.

You'll be sitting patiently, eating your lunch or doing some other absent-minded mundane task, when the musician strikes. No warning as they approach, MP3 player in hand.

Within seconds, you will be at the whim of their fascination with music. Headphones will either be forced upon your head or stuffed into your ears, and music will be blasted so loud into your brain that you get dizzy. It really isn't a fun experience at all.

# "La la la ..."

Not that the music is bad. If you were given the time to ease into it peacefully, you might like it.

But this friend presses their obsession onto you and you don't realise it's growing on you until you're standing at a music concert in the pouring rain, your friend screaming in joy at the singers on the stage, and wondering to yourself: I don't even like this band, how did I get here?

The only way to deal with this musical friend is to go along with it. Listen to whatever music they like because if you don't, they'll make you.

Agree with them on the 'best singer ever' because if you don't, they'll keep going relentlessly until you do. If you smile and nod, you could potentially make it out without (too much) pain.

# SOULMATE

Everyone's heard of the romantically idealised 'soulmate'. The other half to your heart, the one you are meant to be with forevermore. 'Soulmates' are usually couples who are so insecure about their relationship that they try to convince both themselves and their partner that they would not be whole without one another.

But soulmates are not necessarily romantic. You can find people you click with, people which make you wonder if you're adopted and secretly their twin, that's how strong the bond is. This is the person who basically lives at your house and takes up your couch every weekend, who is your parent's favourite – 'Why can't you be more like dear [insertsoulmatesnamehere]?' – and who your dog smothers with affection whenever they take them out for a walk.

The soulmate knows all your secrets. Theirs is the shoulder you cry on when things go wrong, and they always have your back, even when you don't realise you need it. You relate to one another on such a deep level that it seems you were made to be the best of friends.

Plus, they can always make you laugh. What's not to love? At the end of the day, you may never find this person. They might not even exist outside of movies and TV for most of us. But they do exist for some lucky ones, and you often need a best friend like this – a bestie you can really trust.

Depending on your interests, this person might be the avid admirer at all your football matches, always cheering you on at every victory and failure to a point where you are highly motivated and happy. Or they could be the one who helps you pick out an outfit for your first date. Whatever it is, they are always there for you, and you might not even notice it.

In an ideal world, this friend would make you constantly happy and laughing. But this is not an ideal world. You might not realise they're such a good friend until it's too late and you've had some big argument with them and parted company. Friends like this come and go – you need to be careful, and keep the really good ones close. This is a person you want to have as a friend for the rest of your life, potentially.

# SCHOOL WORK
# THE STUDY BUDDY MOMENT

## HOW TO LEARN

I don't look like someone who could lecture you about learning, but... Well, yeah, I'm not someone who could lecture you about learning. Bear with me. I'm only going to lecture you about learning specific things, not just what teachers tell you to learn in class.

You see, it's all very well and good to do the work set. But if you can do it, and the work set for the next week, then you're bound to get some amazing grades. Even if that isn't your main goal, getting good grades is useful, because if you're not worrying about your grades, then you can focus on other things that are more important to you.

So listen up!

I'm going to tell you what you can do in each subject to help you improve at them.

Everyone deserves to feel proud of their grades, even you!

*Keep in mind, I'm no expert. I'm not a teacher. I'm just telling you what I know about each subject so far.*

*So if you find other tips and tricks, be sure to use them as well – and pass them on. Everyone needs a good study buddy to get them through the school system!*

# ENGLISH: THE LIT AND LANGS

For English Lit, it's all about '**why**?' Why did this happen, and not that? If you can say why and use examples, you might up your GCSE grade from a 5 to a 7 or higher.

I'll give you two examples.

*1: 'Romeo and Juliet is a tragedy because everyone dies. End of story.'*

*2: 'Romeo and Juliet is a tragedy because of its copious amounts of death. It depicts the tragic foolish affair of two adolescents as they journey towards adulthood, and shows how the disparaging hatred of two families can create a toxic environment in which death and suicide occur.'*

Okay, not brilliant. But which of those sounds more compelling, 1 or 2?

Whatever your opinion of Shakespeare, you have to study his plays at some point! Try to think of them as stories rather than plays written in ye-olde language, and concentrate on who does what, and most importantly, **why**.

# "Don't forget to P.E.E!"

## POINT, EVIDENCE, EXPLANATION

*Make a POINT about the story or play you're studying.*

*Back your point up with EVIDENCE (like a very short quotation from the play).*

*EXPLAIN what you mean or why you've chosen to make that point or use that quotation.*

In English Language, you also use P.E.E. when talking about texts. But instead of the 'why', it's all about the 'how'. In other words, how does a writer create an effect on the reader? Using what's called 'tropes' like weather or types of settings or characters is how the writer makes the reader feel something.

Remember to use those long words! Get a load of long, difficult words, put them in a blender … and wait for your teacher to stare at you in amazement. Just make sure you know what those long words mean though. Or things can get a bit embarrassing.

# MATHS, OR, SUMZ YOU CAN'T DO

Look, either you love maths or you loathe it.

Many of your classmates will be questioning themselves every day, wondering what maths can actually do for them in the future and cursing it with every possible name under the sun.

Learn the basic rules for different types of maths (algebra, geometry, fractions) before going back in and learning a few more of each until you know most of the ways to do each type of maths, and even if you don't, you can guess them.

Maths is hard even when you have a calculator. Be proud of your skills in maths – the more you struggle to understand something, the better you feel when you finally get it. And maybe you can make friends with a sheep penguin by offering to help them with maths too … Or not.

# MAD SCIENCE

As you probably know, there are three basic sciences: biology, physics and chemistry. Depending on your school, you might have to study one, or two, or all of them, or you might get to choose.

Whatever it is, you'll never be free from science. So why not rule science yourself? Everyone can be good at science if they stay calm and be scientific.

One tip to learning science is to study hard. Not much fun, I agree. But hit the books and work on your technique.

Something useful may be memorising those triangle-thingies. If you want the one on the top then you multiply the two on the bottom. If you want one of the ones on the bottom, you get the one on the top and divide it by the other one on the bottom.

Science is useful for all types of jobs, from cooking all the way to building rockets for NASA. Remember to look to the future!

# MFL, OR, SPRECHEN ZE FRANCAIS?

You'll probably end up learning at least one language in school, be it German, Spanish, French, or whatever. If you can become the master of this language, then you can go to any country in the world where that language is spoken, without having to carry a dictionary with you everywhere. Smooth!

A few phrases to learn that might be useful, just as you get started:

*'My name is ____.'*

*'How are you?'*

*'Do you speak English?'*

*'Where is ____?'*

*'Thank you!'*

*'Can you repeat that, slower, please?'*

*'I don't understand.'*

The easiest way to learn a language is to speak it, listen to it, and read it just about 24/7. How do you think babies learn languages so quick? If you get to go on holiday to a country where your chosen language is spoken, then speak as little English as possible. Difficult, yes, but trust me. It works. Don't be disheartened if you find native speakers are too quick for you to understand. You'll get better. Practice makes perfect.

Even if you don't have the opportunity to go to that country, then do what you can – watch movies in your chosen language without subtitles, and keep pausing and rewinding until you can actually understand what they're saying.

My mum did this with me to help me learn French. I'm certainly not fluent or anything, but it definitely helped a lot when I was first learning. Now I'm not scared even when someone speaks quickly, because I'm used to hearing fast French and I know it's possible to work out what's being said, with a little extra effort.

# LIFE THREATENING SCHOOL SITUATIONS

## MY TOP GUIDE TO WRIGGLING OUT OF TROUBLE

### HOW TO LOOK LIKE YOU KNOW THE ANSWER (WHEN YOU TOTALLY DON'T)

To get through secondary school, you need to be prepared to act cool, even in the trickiest situations.

Let's start off simple. We all have that moment in class when the teacher is talking, and you just find yourself zoning out. Then suddenly –

*'AHEM! What is x if y is 4? Hmm … You!'*

*'Who, me???'*

The teacher's eyes – and everyone else's eyes, even worse – are on you now. In this situation, you have around 5 seconds to answer, before the teacher humiliates you further. First, you have to focus.

If you actually know the answer, then don't sweat it, you're fine. But if you have no clue, there are some routes you could take to avoid more humiliation ...

**Phone a friend** – turn to the person sitting next to you and say, as smoothly and confidently as possible, 'I don't know, how about you?' If you are bold enough, you can look like that's what you were planning all along, not that you're choosing it as a last resort.

**Make it funny** – Turn a simple question about algebra into a joke and everyone can have a laugh, at nobody's expense. This can also increase your popularity, because your classmates and maybe even your teacher might be happy to do something interesting instead of the usual dry routine!!

# THE GREAT HOMEWORK DILEMMA

You walk into class on the first day back after a holiday and you're smug. You did all your homework, you completed that gigantic History project, and everything is good. But the person next to you says, 'Hey, did you do the English homework? Which play did you do?'

Suddenly you're filled with dread – you totally forgot the homework. The doom of being singled out by the teacher, everyone's eyes on you, laughing at your misery, detention, letters home, yet another stain on your record –

Okay, stop right there. **You're overreacting!!!**

So, let's give you an example. The teacher takes the register, and then they stand up. They ask everyone to hand in the homework, and all the other students take theirs to the teacher's desk. After everyone is done, the teacher takes the pile and counts the pieces before pausing. 'Someone has not handed in their homework.'

At this point you have two choices. Either you sit back and wait to be discovered, or you stand up and tell the class that it was you.

'I didn't do the homework!' you tell them, standing up with your arms crossed.

Each person in the room turns their heads to you. 'And why exactly didn't you do it?' the teacher asks.

You can pick any lame old excuse in the book, or you can go full thespian and make up a tragic, tear-jerking story up on the spot.

'Well then,' says the teacher sarcastically, 'I'm sure you won't find it hard to do that homework during lunchtime detention every day for the next week. Now, class, let's get back to work!'

**PHEW!** Now that wasn't so bad, was it?

# THE LUNCHTIME LOAN CRISIS

We all have that one friend who, whenever lunch comes around, find themselves penniless. (*Confession: it's usually me!*) They ask for some money, just a pound, so they can buy food at the cafeteria. But maybe you only have enough money for your own lunch, or a present for your crush, and you don't want to give it up.

## Possible Ways To Deal:

– *The straight no.* 'Shove off! I need this money, and I don't have enough to give you any. Ask someone else!'

– *The apologetic fib.* 'Uh… I don't have any money, sorry! I left it at home.'

– *The yes with menaces.* 'Here, only don't blame me when you get food poisoning!'

– *The substitute yes.* 'Nah, I wouldn't be so cruel as to subject you to cafeteria food. Here, have some of my sandwich.'

Now I'll go through a few possible reactions your friend could have, and the consequences.

'Seriously? Some friend you are. If you aren't even considerable enough to give me a little money? I don't want to be your friend if that's your idea of friendship.' [Consequence: YOU LOSE A FRIEND]

'I saw you counting your money just earlier. Don't lie to me! I really can't trust you, can I?' [Consequence: YOU LOSE THEIR TRUST BECAUSE YOU LIED]

'Thanks. I know, I'll get food poisoning, but what can you do? I have to eat.' [Consequence: THEY ACCEPT YOUR HELP BUT ARE NOT VERY ENTHUSIASTIC]

'Wow! Thanks, this is way better than cafeteria food would've been.' [Consequence: THEY ARE EXCITED AND LOVE YOUR FOOD, BUT WILL NOW ASK YOU FOR FOOD ALL THE TIME]

As you can see, there are no easy ways out in this situation, I'm afraid. Maybe try hiding under the table or running away when you see them coming?

# HAIRY STYLES

People often overlook how a person's hair can be a reflection of their personality and status in a school's social hierarchy. Here is a no-nonsense guide to the hairstyles of girls and boys, and what that can tell you about them.

In general, the tidier and more styled a person's hair is, the more likely they are to be a sheep penguin. This is because sheep penguins care a great deal what people think of them.

I have no idea why they care. I certainly don't. Which is probably why my mum's always chasing me out of the house with a hairbrush in the mornings … [*Note from Indigo's Mum: Yes, and in my slippers too!*]

# GIRLS

## THE WOOKIE LOOKIE

When you see someone with hair in a kind of lump of tangles on their head, it implies they don't care all that much about how people see them.

Your hair is here, there and everywhere. You're beginning to wonder when that bird family will finally vacate their nest in your hair, and you have a giant tuft just sticking up at the back for no good reason. Brush? Ha! What is a 'brush'?

Take a minute to think of the last time you had bad hair. If it's right now, then well done! You have first place for 'bad hair day champion.'

Everyone has off days, but if that day seems to be every day for this person's hair, they fit right into this category.

But, alas, I can't really say much. As I admitted before, I honestly couldn't care less about my hair, so it's very messy the majority of the time.

The reason is because I just don't have time, and I don't feel like I should.

My take is, why spend time making my hair pretty when it doesn't matter? What, will I aggravate some poor soul by looking a mess? Anyone who cares that much about how my hair looks isn't someone I want to hang out with.

## THE BOUNCER

Every person who has long hair ends up having to put it into some kind of up-do at some point – PE and cookery requires you to have your hair out of the way. But there are those girls who perpetually have their hair up in buns and ponytails, which are done up so tightly they look kind of bald. I honestly get confused sometimes.

This semi-bald look is often accompanied by the 'on fleek' eyebrows and long eyeliner wings which make up a particularly dominant personality. This person is prepared to make your life a misery if you get on her bad side. She's most likely a sheep penguin. A plankton or a brainiac wouldn't care about their appearance as much.

Alternatively, you can find the messy ponytail in its natural habitat. This is just a slap-dab hairdo you see on a regular basis from a lot of different people.

From Brainiacs just not caring about their looks too much and focusing on their studies, to the plankton who don't want to stand out too much, but also don't want their hair in their eyes all the time.

Behind every slap-dab ponytail there is a different kind of person, ranging from the moody and sleep-deprived kids who crammed for their test the night before (we all know that feeling) to the people whose dogs ate their homework and their alarm clock didn't work and their uniform was still in the wash and their favourite teacher was ill today and was replaced by a horrid teacher who hates them.

# THE OINK

Anyone who's anyone knows that this hairdo – the 'oink' – should have been left behind in primary school. And yet, we still have those few stragglers who think it's cute to have pigtails.

Yeah, it is cute – on 5-year-olds. When I see 15-year-olds with this hairdo, it feels like a mismatch.

But then, they look so innocent and naïve, it is kinda sweet – it reminds me of my six-year-old nephew when he's doing puppy eyes because he wants ice cream. You just can't say no.

I resist the urge to tell them that, hey, pigtails went out of fashion for you ten years ago, because I don't want to see their entire lives and dreams crushed.

Yep, I'm exaggerating, and yep, I know. Sue me.

Braided pigtails aren't too bad though. At least it's creative. And keeps your fingers busy while you're daydreaming in maths …

Once, one of my friends asked what my least favourite type of movie was. I said that it was kids' movies, because they're often tacky, poorly done and not very cool – they just seem kind of silly. This is the same for pigtails. (Yes. I'm using an extended metaphor-thingy. Don't judge, we learned about this in English and I want to sound smart…) They're fun and a bit old-fashioned. But no one's going to take you seriously if you wear your hair like that all the time.

# THE EMO QUEEN

You know those dogs with long hair over their eyes – Old English Sheepdogs - the ones where you keep on questioning how on earth they can function without their eyesight? Why they don't bump into things or fall down stairs? Yeah, this hairstyle is the human version of that.

When someone is so shy that they don't want to be seen, they go by the idea that if THEY can't see you, YOU can't see them. With hair falling over their eyes, these people just blend in with the crowd.

They have to be able to see, of course, so usually it is only one eye covered. I just wonder how those people who cover both eyes get to see the board in class. Though if I had this hairstyle I would take advantage of that in many a class, for certain!

I'm not sure why, but I've recently noticed the increasing popularity – at least in my school – of really long, untameable hair. I think it's honestly pretty cool. It reminds me of the sea, the way it looks with really long hair. I envy all the girls who can whirl their luscious locks around and have a potential weapon, as well.

Knocking everyone out as they go … !

There was this one girl in my class with super-long hair sitting next to me, and there was a pen on the desk. The people behind us were talking, and she turned around to tell them to shut up. But the pen got caught in her incredibly long hair and hit the girl behind us in the face. Not so funny for the person behind us, who was clutching their face and glaring at us for the rest of the lesson.

But we all sniggered like crazy people.

It's kind of a running gag in my friendship group now – *Hair can be deadly, people! Beware the hair!*

Sometimes you can end up at the wrath of such long hair. For instance, if you're running a track race in PE and are right behind a person with long hair, you won't be able to see a thing ahead!

Or you could be in the middle of a dangerous science experiment when their long hair catches fire, despite them putting it up in a ponytail!

Just imagine the headline: 'School burned down because of long hair!' Not a fun way to go, I tell you now.

Interestingly, long hair is not particularly attributed to any specific group of people. From sheep penguin to plankton, you'll probably find this hair style everywhere.

# THE MAGICAL PIXIE

This is t complete contrast to the last one – the pixie bob. It's a hairstyle rising in popularity though, and one which directly contradicts the rise in popularity of long hair!

It confuses me how they can both be 'in fashion' when they're so completely different.

Pixie bobs are often accompanied by dyed hair and a confident, clever attitude.

You'll probably find a few Sheep Penguins with this hairstyle, because it's so bold and exciting that they draw attention to themselves.

When I was younger, I thought pixie bobs were SO COOL. Sad, I know. What can I say?

I was absolutely obsessed and would always draw people with pixie bobs in my doodles. When my friends saw my drawings they were all like, 'where's the hair?' and I would get super embarrassed and tell them the person just had short hair. I wasn't very good at drawing in those days, so I can understand why they would think that, ha!

Anyway, some of my best friends have had pixie bobs. They're so awesome, but I would never have one myself. I'm too attached to my hair. Though I suppose that everyone is literally attached to their hair! Ha! Get it?

Listen, I hope you appreciate those who are confident enough to go for such a spunky look as the short pixie bob. Unlike me. Because I'm not confident.

I'm just really jealous of those who are. That's it, I've admitted it!

# BOYS

## THE AU NATURELLE

In other words, 'this is what it looked like when I got out of bed.' Nice, very nice, boys. (NOT.) This is a common hairstyle on my brother, who stays asleep for as long as possible before suddenly getting everything ready in a mad flurry of activity.

This hairstyle shows just how rushed and disorganised the boys who wear it are. They don't care to do anything with their hair, so just leave it as it is. Unless, of course, they're partaking in a new fashion trend which is to spend hours styling your hair just for it to look messy at the end.

# SONIC THE HEDGEHOG

These pointy spikes of hair could be deadly if you ever head-butted someone. 'Hey, watch out! You could take an eye out with that!' Artificially spiked hair, laced with hair gel, often in vivid colours like a neon dance party, and sometimes even stuck up in a Mohawk. This what you can expect with this hairstyle.

Anyone with this hairstyle is probably broke. The rate at which they use up hair gel makes perfect hair an expensive habit. They may also be constantly in trouble with teachers, because for some reason teachers don't take too kindly to neon hair!

## PERFECTION

Every morning, this boy wakes up at 5am. Not because he has to do something important, but because he has to style his hair. A quiff that can stand up by itself, fluffy tufts of hair at the back, and comb in hand, this guy's hairdo is finally complete by the time 7am rolls around and they can actually get ready for school. As long as putting on his uniform won't muss up his perfect locks, that is.

This type is easily influenced. Sheep penguins are the only ones who'd go to such lengths for a hairdo – is he trying to impress someone?

# TO SPORT OR NOT TO SPORT
### SORRY, NO CHOICE

## 'P.E' ARE THE CHAMPIONS

Everyone knows that PE is (sadly) compulsory – you have to do it and you have no choice on the matter. But if you want to keep fit, you'll have to go to a club as well.

Here are some of the sporting clubs you could attend ... and what to look out for there.

# FOOTBALL

# (NOT FACEBALL, THANK YOU VERY MUCH)

*Football Club* … This is a whole community within itself.

You have the super competitive types who practise for hours every day; the casual footers who aren't too bad; you have the bored crew who only joined because their parents forced them to …

And then you have the useless ones who are so bad that every time they try to kick a ball it ends up landing behind them.

Erm, that would be me.

But at least the rules aren't too hard in football. You kick the ball, and try to get it in the opposite team's goal.

Simple, right?

Yet I assure you, you'll never come out of a football match unscathed.

Everyone's pushing and shoving for the ball, and when they do get it, they hit it so hard it flies and hits you in the face.

**OUCH!!!!**

# ~~MILITARY TRAINING~~ CROSS COUNTRY

If you don't find the idea of football enticing, then you might decide to join the cross country club instead, or the running club, depending on what your school offers. Cross Country is roughly the same as running, right?

**WRONG!!!!!**

I tell you this with many years' experience. Having been to many different schools, I have determined that running and exercise in general should be avoided. Especially the cross country club. Training with the cross country club is simple. You constantly run around. That's it. It is not, though, easy. Neither is it particularly enjoyable.

I remember one time when the teacher running the club made us keep jogging laps, even though it was hailing and we were freezing our butts off in nothing but sodden T-shirts and gym shorts.

Another time, when I lived in deep countryside with green fields and cows everywhere, we ran in the field right beside the school.

Now this was okay, but we also ran in the field next to it – which was so steep, it felt like running up a mountain. We had to dash up to the very top, sprint around the perimeter past a field with some very menacing-looking cows, then slog back around.

Honestly, now that I think about it, that was more like military training or boot camp than a cross country club.

We even went to competitions – all of which I got last place in, despite consistently coming to the club every week for all the years I went to that school – and we had to compete against other kids from schools nearby. All of whom had even steeper fields next to their schools, by the way they charged around with calf muscles like iron.

I'm telling you, it was brutal.

## JOLLY HOCKEY STICKS

I never used to go to hockey club at primary school. It seemed even more brutal than cross country. But after my disastrous experience with running and a few horror stories about my new school's cross country team, I decided to choose hockey once I started at secondary.

Now for a basic rundown of hockey for those who don't know the sport. You have a stick, which you use to push the ball around. It's not allowed to hit your foot.

You aren't allowed to have two people gang up on one person in a tackle. (Because that would be mean, natch!) Most importantly, you aren't allowed to lift your stick above your waist.

These rules exist for a reason. For instance, regardless of however many times the other team aggravates you, you are not allowed to whack any of them in the head. You might break your stick.

I'd like to draw your attention to how aggressive people can get when playing a game of hockey. I can't fathom it. I'm not innocent either, I think there's some kind of curse on the game because everyone who plays it seems unable to control their inner rage. Maybe that's why people play it, to let it all out on the field so they can act like a human being later.

If you don't know what I'm talking about, I'll give you an example. We were playing a game of hockey, and I had no idea how hard I was trying to win until the teacher told me off for tackling someone so violently that I accidentally chipped their hockey stick.

**Soooo embarrassing!!!**

# BULLYING

Okay, here's how it goes. Everyone's had to sit through that long assembly about bullying. Everyone's had to engage in that PSHE class about bullying. But not everyone's had to see and experience first-hand the effects of bullying.

It's what everyone's terrified of. Bullying. You get assemblies about it shoved in your face throughout your school life from the moment you're able to read, and everyone knows abut it. Social ridicule? The rejection of your peers? I'm with you all on this one… Bullying is pretty terrifying.

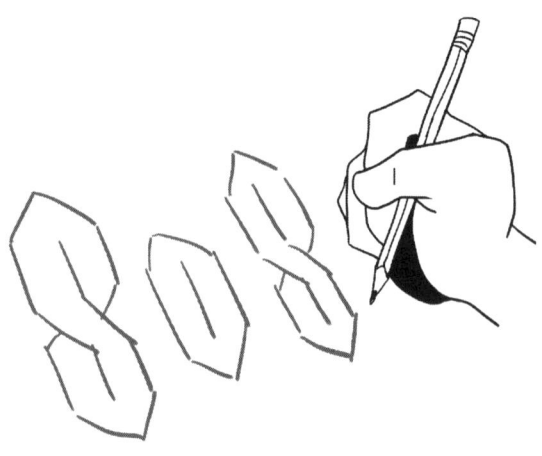

There are many different types of bullying, so don't treat every type you see the same. One thing I won't mention is cyber bullying, but with cyber bullying you can go through the same process you would for any other type of bullying.

The difference? **Online, you can block and report people.**

# YOUR DAILY DOSE OF ... A PUNCH IN THE FACE

Three things to know about physical bullying.

*1. This is the bullying variety you hear about most, mainly because it's a big red flag for the staff and it gets pupils suspended.*

*2. This is one type of bullying you're less likely to receive from a girl, though it can happen, and I know a few friends who've gone through it.*

*3. You often find the victims of violent bullying are unlikely to tell someone else what's happening ... often until it's too late.*

If someone's picking on you physically, you may not want to look vulnerable by admitting it.

For most people, their pride is the most important thing, and they don't like to risk looking weak. Which means we have to be vigilant as a school community and spot when it's happening, then report it on behalf of the victim.

It's not your job to worry about what makes a bully behave the way they do. Just stick to reporting them.

## BULLYING TIP:
### Never punch the bully back.

Don't get into a fight because then you run the risk of stooping to their level. Don't resort to physical violence, you're better than that!

### Tell the principal or head teacher.

Not just the teacher on hand at the time, who may have missed what happened.

But don't turn a blind eye when you see something wrong going down at school. Imagine it's happening to your little brother or sister, or to you. Wouldn't you want someone to stand by you and get the bully reported?

# A MUCH DEEPER, INVISIBLE KIND OF PAIN

Psychological bullying is when people hurt your feelings rather than your body, but can be just as hurtful as a punch in the face. Maybe more so, as bruises heal quickly while internal wounds may never entirely heal.

Psychological damage can be pretty horrifying, even to someone completely disconnected from the situation and just looking in.

But the real horror is seeing it first-hand and knowing you should be helping to prevent it, but aren't.

When a bully sees someone better than them in some way, they want to drag them down. Down to their own level, before pushing them even further down, so far down they feel like they have no hope of getting back up.

Many bullies don't need fists to do this. However unbelievable it may be, bullies can also use their brains to ruin people's lives.

Everyone has that nagging feeling that they could do better, that they aren't good enough.

But someone in real life telling you that you're ugly, stupid, useless, or fat is bringing it to a new level of horror.

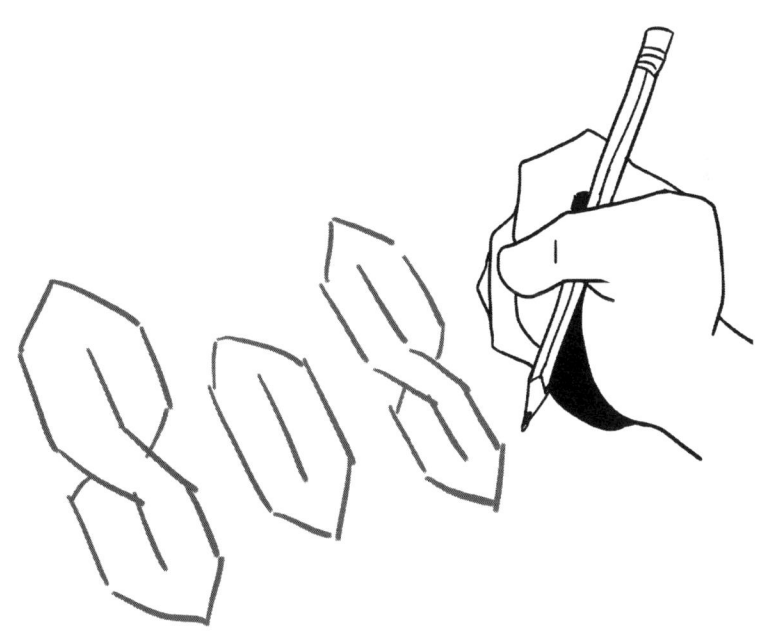

A bully will tell their victim things which are hurtful, but simply aren't true:

'You think you're clever? Well you're not. You smell. You look awful too. You're thick as two planks. You're the worst. Your parents must be ashamed to have given birth to you.'

At this point, you could say, 'I don't think it's physically possible for two people to give birth to one baby. I'm pretty sure only one of them was actually going through *labour*. Though I suppose you wouldn't know since you never pay attention in Biology.'

But that rebuke is hard to come up with on the spot, especially when you're surrounded and you're probably on the verge of crying from all the other horrible things they said.

Just stay calm. And report them.

It's not very nice, being bullied like this. That's an understatement, of course. So never sit by and watch without helping while someone else is being bullied.

Would you want someone to help you when you're being bullied? You would, naturally.

What goes around comes around, my friend. One day in the future, Karma will bite you in the butt if you don't help them now. And plus – it's the right thing to do.

(Karma means destiny or fate, by the way, for those of you still scratching your heads. And it's not a curry. That's a Korma.)

# KEEP CLEAN, KEEP SAFE
### and *keeeeeeep dancing!!*

# A GUIDE TO TEACHERS

## ABSOLUTE EDUCATORS

With teachers, there is no in-between. There is only 'absolute'. Teachers can be absolutely horrible or absolutely amazing. They can't be kind of horrible or kind of amazing. That's how they work. As extremes. When you are looking for teachers to be wary of, it will always be the ones who try to be 'kind of' but fail miserably, resulting in mood swings and obvious hypocrisy.

For example, our first one …

# THE ABSOLUTE CONTROLLER

I understand that teaching can be very stressful. Teenagers aren't the easiest people to deal with, and I know this from personal experience, having two brothers! (Plus, teachers have tons of paperwork too and aren't paid very much.)

The problem is, sometimes I have to wonder why some teachers chose teaching as their preferred profession.

The **Absolute Controller** is not an easy teacher to negotiate with …

Homework is set – and it's due the very next day. You don't have it with you for next lesson?

*"Immediate detention. You had 'plenty of time'. What, you only wrote a page? Redo it, not good enough. You should've written at least 5 pages."*

Trying to reason with Absolute Controllers is hard but not unheard of. Maybe they'll have an epiphany – a sudden realisation – and decide to change their ways. (Yeah, right.)

There's a good part of all of us, and if you discover a way to help your teacher see that, then by all means, show them.

Often they'll hate telling you off as much as you hate being told off.

It can be aggravating and seem like you're getting nowhere, but be patient. They could surprise you and turn around eventually. Try as hard as possible not to incur their wrath, and keep hoping.

Never give up.

# THE ABSOLUTE BEST TEACHER EVER!

This is the complete opposite of the controller. The ideal teacher. If you try hard enough, you can convince an Absolute Controller to become like this. They are considerate of the feelings of their students. They don't try to scare them. They try to nurture their natural talent and help them blossom into a person who ... gets good grades.

Now don't get me wrong. Achieving good grades is a noble goal. But is it really all they want in the world?

This teacher's catchphrase is, 'I'm just really trying hard to help you get your target grade!' There's nothing beyond that, it seems, and nobody can tell them any better. This is because, as you can tell, the test results negate everything else. Anyone they teach gets their target grade.

This teacher is basically worshipped by Brainiacs. (I think they have temples and everything.) When they tell you to do something, you do it.

Most people want good grades, and this teacher is the master of achieving your target grade, so they are wise to anything you need to do in order to get an A or even an A*.

If you so much as speak a word against this teacher, the Brainiacs will wonder how on earth you could think such a mean thing because they're just so perfect and kind and they always help you out when you need it.

But whatever wacky method of teaching they have in store for us, it does seem to help some people out. So I guess I should just shut up and learn.

Sigh …

# THE ABSOLUTE ECCENTRIC

Everyone's a bit weird on the inside. Some of us like TV a tad too much – not pointing any fingers! – and some of us really like clicking their ballpoint pen in a quiet classroom. Continuously. In a really annoying manner. I mean, seriously? Who does that? WHO? (I'm looking at you, ballpoint pen-clicking teacher.) Whatever you feel is weird about you, trust me, this teacher is ten times weirder.

This teacher may keep gross plants like Venus Fly Traps in their classroom. And ask you to call them by their first name like you're best buds!

They eat lunch in their room and leave all their plates and debris out so that their desk is constantly piled high with things which they should've returned to the canteen weeks ago. Along with the plants, this causes a ton of flies to swarm round the classroom in the summer. This teacher will also stare. And stare. And stare … Not at you but into the distance.

You begin to wonder if someone out there has fainted, given how intensely they're staring out the window or at the back of the classroom.

Next, they'll make a seating plan where you have to sit down next to your worst enemies - and end up bickering every five seconds. It's as though they get a kick out of making their students feel uncomfortable and miserable!

These teachers are so, so, so very strange. I think they're secretly from Mars.

Perhaps we should warn the government …

# THE ABSOLUTE GATEKEEPER

Is it rude to call these teachers archaic? You're supposed to 'respect your elders' and all that (as most teachers will constantly remind you) but there's honestly nothing more annoying, yet at the same time more hilarious, than an older teacher who reminds you about the 'good old days'. But they're more of a gatekeeper, so I'll call them that.

These teachers will smile at you. A lot.

But you'll know it's fake because their eyes will have this glaring expression at the same time, and what they're saying is far from cheery. Their charm is very subtle though. Like magic.

Many parents have fallen under their spell at Parents' Evenings …

Teens see right through the act because rather than assuming adults are nice, teens tend to assume they are bad. Or maybe they simply don't notice because they're too busy playing the latest game on their phone or texting someone two rows behind.

That phone time will be short-lived though. Because the second the gatekeeper teacher sees you with any type of technology, they screech and confiscate it.

*'In the good old days, we didn't have these stupid devices to distract adolescents! You should be paying attention to me, not a screen!' etc etc.*

**Yadayadayada ...**

Trust me, you'll never get that phone back without serious work. The gatekeeper guards their hoards of confiscated items like a dragon guards its piles of gold.

You'll have to say the magic word – 'please' –then learn a new language – 'the polite language of the gatekeeper'. This can take a while. And lots of smiles.

A few of you (i.e. parents) will be thinking, it's justified, right? They are students and shouldn't be playing on their phones.

They should be learning.

This teacher can't be that bad, right?

**UM, WHATEVER.**

But confiscating phones is just the beginning. Trust me, **I KNOW.**

These older teachers will have very little idea about computers. Every lesson ends up like teaching your grandparents how to use the world wide interwebz. "Yes, you push THIS button and then ... hey presto, the "email" has been sent. Honest!"

Of course, if you try to help, to hurry things along, they'll tell you to sit down because they have decided they can handle it.

While you wait, bored out of your skull, people chitter-chat ... and of course, the teacher tells *you* off. The one who offered to help, because you're nearest and their fading eyesight can't focus on anything further than three rows in.

So they give *you* the detention, even though you weren't the one who was talking.

**GRRRRRRRR.**

# THE WET-BEHIND THE EARS NQT

Everyone has to start somewhere. It's simply unfortunate that when teachers start out – as the NQT or Newly Qualified Teacher – they are too often young, naïve and seem astonishingly uninformed in the ways of teens. Especially considering they are still only a few years off teenagerhood themselves, that is.

Powerpoints are fun. Yes? They're pretty cool. Agreed?

But when the whole lesson is simply reading off a Powerpoint, it's exactly like we're still in the bad old days (see Gatekeeper teacher above) when we read silently from textbooks. But no one will complain. Oh no. Because this teacher will bend over backwards to make their students like them.

They'll bring cake and sweets to class every week so they can bribe you into becoming friends with them – and not moaning about the interminable boredom that is Death By Powerpoint.

Not that I'm complaining about food bribery. Cake and sweets are tasty. But it's hard to concentrate when the whole class is shouting all around you in some strange satanic-like ritual of worshipping the cake. They chant things like 'Cake! Cake! Cake!' over and over again in unison, and so loudly that you get a migraine. Then, as if this wasn't appalling enough, you are bludgeoned over the head with a Powerpoint lesson.

Cakes and Powerpoint lessons are okay on their own, right? Well, not exactly okay, but they aren't valid reasons to hate a teacher. Of course, 'hate' is a strong word. But so is 'love'. And I'm pretty sure that almost half your classmates will be swooning for this teacher, for the simple reason that they are no more than 10 years older than us. Plus, they give out cake. *Ewww.*

But I shouldn't complain. That makes the lessons easier, because you don't have to do anything challenging. You can just relax and watch people get covered in cake crumbs and gibber and make utter fools of themselves.

# FRIENDSHIP GROUPS

A friendship group is like a miniature fanatical cult where you're all competing to impress the cult leader, the sheep penguin of the group. Having more than one sheep penguin in a friendship group can spell trouble, as it may crack and shatter. Like my parents' favourite vase that time I bumped into it when playing tag with my brothers. There was a lot of crying and shouting that day too.

**WATCH OUT FOR THAT VASE!!!!**

# THE DEMONIC DAISY CHAIN

This group tries so hard to be all sunshine and daisy chains. But, in the end, it's more like a dysfunctional family where the parents worship demons and try to get their kids to do the same.

This group is constantly shattering – and then regrouping. Their main fault lies with the sheer amount of sheep penguins in the group.

It's many subgroups mish-mashed together to create an amalgamation of terror and chaos.

They have no specific group leader, because they're constantly competing to try and become the group leader.

Every other day a new person will have gained power.

# THE AMBITIOUS SPORTS GROUP

Sports are important, even vital to the school community. I just sometimes wish whoever decided that sports were mandatory in school would die a tragic, horrid death. The people in this friendship group believe vehemently otherwise.

Their natural habitat? The sports hall. The football pitch. The school gym. It's not too hard to find them, with their love for all things sporty. They just love to do sports. Everything they do is linked to sports. I can't imagine doing that – but maybe I'm just lazy! I'd much prefer to read a book than run a mile.

Are you prepared to exercise for two hours a day? If you want to become one of them, have a go! It's a tightly-knit community where they celebrate health and exercise. They are loyal and will have your back.

If you're planning to do a run for charity or something, then the Sports Group will be there for you. They'll help you raise triple what you would've raised by yourself. This is simply one scenario when being in this friend group will help you to help others.

And help yourself – keeping fit is an honourable goal, and everything is easier when you have a group of friends supporting you.

Rest assured, if you become one of them then you'll have to fully commit. Find a sport team which you tin are doing well, and support it.

It'll be more fun, if you buy some of the team's merchandise, because who doesn't want a scarf with their favourite team's colours, right?

It feels great to be a part of a community. But don't try to fake it, you have to really get into it. Honesty is the best policy, remember!

# THE ETERNAL DARKNESS GROUP

Whenever Halloween comes around, things get creepy in school. People organise creepy Halloween parties. People buy creepy Halloween costumes. It really does begin to have an air of creepiness. Now imagine if this was happening all year round.

These worshippers of eternal darkness like to stay in the darkest classrooms possible during lunch, chewing mournfully on something dark and bad for you like chocolate. Though they might drift into the library occasionally, to embrace the darkness quietly in a corner, perhaps, or scan the shelves for paranormal fiction. Yay for creepiness.

Take a deep breath, by the way, and hold it. You have to hold your breath while you walk past these groupies, as they might infect you with the deepest lamentation they ooze from every pore.

And now for a big but … (That's but, not butt.) This could be your chance to make friends who might actually be PROPER FRIENDS instead of fake friends who are just looking for gossip, so I'd encourage you to accept this challenge with the utmost vigour and determination. You might as well, and hey, it'll probably be more fun than some of your other choices.

To be friends with them, you'll need to understand how they feel. Listen to some songs that they like and you'll really get it.

Once they open up they're really nice people. Some of my greatest friends have been what you could classify as members of the 'Eternal Darkness' friend group.

They're understanding and always willing to listen, so go out there and you won't regret being one of their friends!

# THE EXTREME STUDY GROUP

I told you earlier to study, study, study like your life depends on it! Take a wild guess at what I'm about to tell you to do. Come on, give it a go. Three guesses, two don't count.

Study, study, study like your life depends on it! It is pretty vital, of course, since failing all your classes won't exactly help you in your quest to survive school. What, studying is boring? What, studying is even more boring because you have no friends in your class to study with?

Yessssssss! This is the long-awaited chapter on how to become part of a study group …

Study Club will likely be involve younger kids. Older kids are too caught up doing strange, teenager things like ogling visiting sports teams while younger kids still believe in intellectual study. They're innocent and naïve, in other words, with no idea how unlikely it is they'll still value intelligent conversation when they're 15.

They're easy to find – normally in the library – and easy to chat with, because you know exactly why they're there. You can ask what they're studying and their opinion of it. And they'll be happy to share information, with accuracy and enthusiasm, unlike older teens who might just shrug and go, 'Whatever.'

The same people will come to a study group every time, without fail. So, within a short time, you can become a part of this small but dedicated community, gaining knowledge skills as you study alongside them. Very useful!!

# THE INCREDIBLE JOURNEY!

How you get to school can greatly impact your experience of what happens once you arrive.

If you walk, then obviously you must live closer to school – unless you're some kind of super-athlete – and that can have an impact on how you view the institution where you learn.

If you go to school on the bus or even train, you'll probably be travelling with other kids at the same school or other schools nearby, which could change the reach of your social circle.

# THE WHEELS ON THE BUS ...

If you go on the bus to school, you obviously don't exactly live right next door. Public or school transport to and from school each day is a very... social experience.

First things first, it's *loud* on the bus. However much the bus driver tries to shut them all up, you will still find yourself crammed next to rude boys, or the pair who are disgustingly snogging in the back of the bus while everyone tells them to get a room, or the girls who are breaking up their friendship group with a screaming catfight in the seats right in front of you. The only upside about the bus is the fact that you make friends with people you normally wouldn't because of your shared experiences every day. A lot of bonding happens in the worst of situations.

# WALKING
## THE PASSIONATE PURSUIT OF HEALTH (WHICH USUALLY FAILS)

Every day, your parents will tell you the same kind of thing – 'Remember to exercise and eat healthily!' If they don't, then you're lucky.

The news stories about how you have to eat a certain amount of fruit and vegetables every day and such gets their brains thinking that they're bad parents for not enforcing a healthy lifestyle upon their child/children.

Being forced to walk to school can be a symptom of this kind of healthy thinking. (Unless you live really nearby, because then it's just common sense, of course. No point hopping on a school bus for all of, oh, thirty seconds to the gate.)

Walking to school is convenient too, because you get to wake up at least half an hour later than everyone who takes the bus. More time for zzzz … yay!

This can be a bad thing sometimes though. If I had a pound for every time I've had to shout at my brothers to hurry up because we have two minutes until the first lessons start and we live five minutes' walk from the school, then I would have enough money to pay them to wake up earlier so we don't have the problem in the first place!

Also, do not underestimate the bitter cold of winter or the harsh hail of April showers. Too many times have I had to use my bag as an umbrella on the way home from school because it was deceptively sunny in the morning, so I didn't bring a coat.

At least as a walker-to-school, your life is just as flexible as that pesky weather. If you want to go early, you can go early. If you get afterschool detention, you don't have to worry about calling your parents to pick you up. You can just walk home late and pretend that you had a club or something. (Damn, I think my mum just spotted me writing that. Now I'm in trouble ...) (*Indigo's Mum: yes, you are. And watch your language!*)

# 'ARE WE THERE YET?'

It's a cliché in children's books that the kids always go 'Are we there yet?' on a car ride. Honestly, it's more likely your parents will be the ones asking that. If you're in that annoying zone where it's too far to walk to school, but not far enough that you can go on the bus, then you'll just have to stick with … travelling by car.

As your parents will tell you endlessly, they have to go to work, they aren't just there to chaperone you to and from school like your personal chauffeur!

Worse still, your parents will constantly be worrying as they drive you in, and asking you questions …

*Have you got your lunch?* ✓

*Correct uniform?* ✓

*Homework and books?* ✓

Basically, the best thing you can do at this point is keep silent. Anything you say will be taken the wrong way.

"What, you're staying at school late? Did you get a detention?" "No, Mum. I've got a club tonight." And then comes the glare and the infamous, 'You never told me about *that*!'

This is usually after you've mentioned it several times, brought a slip home for your parents to sign, maybe even got them to pay something towards it …

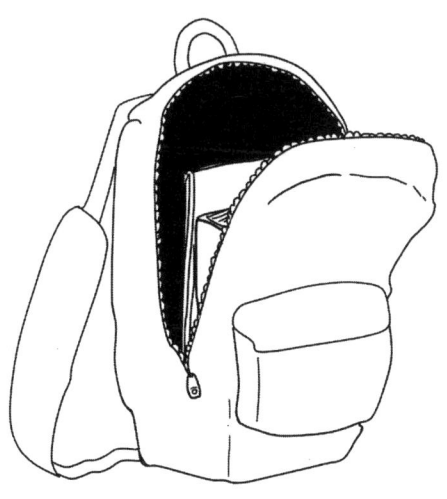

If you see one of your friends on the way to school, there's that really awkward moment when you try to wave to them but they don't see you, so you just keep waving until the person next to them, who you don't know, notices and looks at you funny because you're smiling, staring and waving at them.

Finally, you realise that your car has passed them by and there's no point waving anymore.

And finally, you're here. You step out of the vehicle, but not before your parent bombards you with questions, making sure you'll be okay.

It's like a reverse of your first day at school, when you were latching onto their leg and pleading them not to go.

Parents are SO WEIRD sometimes.

# ARE YOU AN EARLY BIRD OR A NIGHT OWL?

I remember once hearing that early birds scientifically have a better day than a night owl. It's probably true. But honestly, I couldn't care less if going to bed at 10 in the evening and waking up at 6 am is a better idea. I'll keep going to bed at midnight. I mean, if I wake up at 8 am, that's still 8 hours, right?

I'm not failing at school just because I stay up an extra two hours and sleep in an extra two hours. Sadly, teachers seem to want to shove their sleepist propaganda down our throats. *Sleep longer! Go to bed earlier!* Honestly, I couldn't care less. Why don't they worry about their own sleep cycles, and leave us to drool on our desks during the boring parts of their lessons?

Wow, I am such a bad influence. I should probably fix that. ☺

Whatever I think, your teachers will certainly like you better if you don't show up for class half-asleep because you accidentally slept in and didn't have time to get yourself coffee or whatever your morning poison is. I've had one or two shameful moments when I've walked in literally a few seconds late to a class, and my teacher is glaring at me like I just ran over their puppy. Everyone else is, of course, already seated and writing down the date in their books.

*Oops, am I late? My bad.*

Personally, I always blame my brothers for lateness. Like a default. That's what brothers are for, isn't it?

On the other hand, being early to school can be dull. I remember one time I was early; it was horrific. I had to sit in the library twiddling my thumbs until the bell rang. And I still got the teacher glare thing, because I took too long to walk across to my class and everyone else was already sitting down! Sometimes, you can't win …

# KEEPING UP WITH THE "-ISMS"

Okay, here we go with the –isms. What do you expect here? A rant about **sexism, racism, homophobia, perhaps**?

These issues certainly need to be dealt with, and are particularly potent in a school environment where rowdy teens are impressionable and narcissistic.

But that's not what I'm talking about here. Instead, I'll show you all the –isms you never even imagined could effect your school day.

# LUNCHISM

Remember I advised you to bring your own lunch to school, to spare yourself the expense and unknown qualities of cafeteria food? Well, as insane as it might seem, that lunch choice is going to define and limit your social status.

If you have some sandwiches and an apple, you aren't exactly going to be energised for the day ahead. But at least you'll survive the kind of ridicule or awe you get when you bring in a strange exotic food for your lunch.

*Sushi? So cool! Gimme some, I love raw fish!*

*Caesar salad with croutons? Urgh! What are you, a bunny rabbit?*

Basically, you never know what reaction people will have to your packed lunch.

I honestly don't care what your lunch consists of. What you eat is none of my business. Take a wild guess what lunch I bring in? A sandwich, a fruit or two, and a breakfast bar. That's it. Not very imaginative. But really, does it matter?

Apparently to teens, it does matter. And don't even send me off on the subject of the ridicule you'll garner if you **don't** have cafeteria fish and chips on a Friday at our school.

Dunno how it is at your school, but Friday is the one day you are not allowed to miss school dinners. It's just super weird if you have packed lunch when you could have fish and chips.

Tradition, man. It's gotta be done.

# CLUBISM

The sports in which you partake are vital. (Not.) But there is more to life than sport. (Thankfully!)

At any school, you'll find a wide range of after school clubs which do not involve sport. From chess (is chess a sport?) to choir, and from drama to art, you should have a lot of choice, and if you do have a fondness for sport clubs there are those ones as well. Enjoy!

If you go to chess club, you'll make some great Brainiac friends. Chess is also a great way to make your brain work, while also playing and having fun! Doesn't that seem awesome?

Of course, whatever club you choose, there will be people who judge you for that choice, and for the people you hang out with. There's no helping it. So make your choice and embrace the bad with the good.

So which clubs do popular people frequent? If you go to a club with popular people, then surely they'll like you more, right? Wrong. It's a much better idea to go join a more niche cub, because the people there will be having a lot of fun.

There is no definitive way to deal with clubism. Even if you tell them to shut up and mind their own business, they won't do it. You just need to have the satisfaction of knowing that you're having fun. That's the point of joining a club, right? To have fun!

So it doesn't matter what they think, don't let them get to you.

# BRAINISM

If you study like your life depends upon it, then you'll end up achieving great things.

But the problem is, people who see anyone cleverer than them will naturally feel a little jealous. Well, more than a little. The flame of jealousy will be alight within them because you are cleverer than them.

A fire needs three things to survive. Heat, oxygen and fuel. The heat is their mindset. The thinking of, 'If someone's better than me, I should bring them down so they're on the same level as me.' The fuel is the fact that you're clever, and the oxygen is… I don't know.

So either you act like you aren't clever, wasting your potential, or you have to ignore it and try not to care that they hate you.

Never give up the one thing that makes you human – your brain. Brains are things which still elude and confuse scientists because of their complexity. Your brain, your dreams, your emotions… all of those things make you human. Do not try to be something you're not. Don't give up on your dreams for others!

As I said earlier, you can try and reason with them. Convince them. Everyone deserves to feel smart, but you can't help it if your very existence makes others feel like they aren't smart. The only thing you can do is support and encourage them. They hate you for the fact that your brain works differently to theirs, but you can't change that. All you can do is try and convince them to make themselves feel better by becoming better – not by making others worse.

Ignore the nay-sayers and go conquer the world with your brain. You can do it.

# Afterword – A few last tips

So you've discovered the secrets of dealing with teachers, you've studied sheep penguins in their natural habitat, met the brainiacs and all the other crazed students, joined every sports club going, and now you've snuck your way into the top spot in the majority of your maths, science and English classes.

So, what now? How will any of this knowledge and information help you as a newly-fledged adult?

Short answer, it won't. But it will achieve one thing right now. It will make you stand out. And stand out enough to survive school. Life at secondary school can be a dreary succession of repetitive tasks, meandering from one day to the next. Unless you inject your life with some excitement and challenge, you might just die of sheer boredom.

Right there at your desk in Year 9 Geography.

So every morning when you wake up, think this to get you through: 'Someday I'll be free and won't have to deal with these mountains of homework.'

Repeat as required. It could take years. Sorry.

Alright, I'll be serious. You've made it this far, I might as well congratulate you for reading this whole book (and myself for writing it. It was a life and death struggle at times, I can tell you.)

### Now I'll give you some REAL advice.

In 10 years, school will be nothing but a memory. Talking about your school days will be as embarrassing and amusing as when your parents show your friends baby pictures.

But it will also be sweetly nostalgic. You may even begin to wonder what all those sheep penguins are doing as adults…

# "Standing out ..."

Meanwhile, don't let yourself be swallowed by the tide of everyday survival. Don't accept other people's values as your own. Always question what you're told. (Even question this book. Yes, that's the spirit.)

It's important to stand up for who you are deep-down inside. Dare to ask questions. Insist on being different.

When you're different, you stand out. Trust me on this. And once you do, your life will change. So get comfortable with that idea.

It's not always easy to stand out, but it sure beats being invisible.

Teachers will ask your opinion and use your work as a gold standard for other students.

And why would teachers do that? Because you **STAND OUT**. And you yourself will have made that choice to stand out, not to hide or pretend you're not special.

Ultimately you'll never escape school. (Not unless you leave formal education and start being home-educated or 'educated otherwise' than at school – as I've been, several times in the past – or until you're beyond the age of compulsory education.)

But you can decide not to let school eat you alive and cramp your style!

Eventually, people will start to wave at you and say 'hi' as you walk past like you're old friends (even if you have to pause for a moment because you have no idea who that person is). You'll get invited for sleepovers and birthday parties and everyone will know your name.

Listen, there will always be popular people and unpopular people at school. There will also be people who stand out in your memory when you look back on your school days. Just like you occasionally remember stand-out friends you knew at primary school and wonder whatever happened to them.

Those people who stand out at secondary school are not necessarily the ones who are uber-popular. Sometimes they're the people who get picked last for sports, or wear odd clothes, or dance kookily at the school disco. The people others aren't sure they understand. The people who read books for pleasure. (I mean, who does THAT? *COUGH* Me... *COUGH*)

But whatever people say about them, those 'different' people always seem to be going somewhere. Somewhere you'd rather like to be going too. Somewhere ... **special.**

So if you only take one message away from this guide to surviving the secondary school experience, let it be this, and keep referring back to it as you go through your years at school …

**ALLOW YOURSELF TO BE SPECIAL!**

I myself have not finished surviving secondary school, but I'll tell you this… I'm not merely going to survive my school days, but live every one of them to the full.

Because I'm different.

I stand out, no matter what other people think of me or say about me.

Now it's your turn. Good luck, friend.

*Indigo Haynes*

Printed in Great Britain
by Amazon